To my husband and children who love me through the seasons of life and help me to discover true ~~joy~~.

Kindness: Vol. 1
Copyright © 2023 by Amber Joy Thaxton
ISBN: 979-8-218-12217-1

Printed in the United States of America
Design by goldmill.co

Published by Joseph's Ministry, LLC
www.josephsministryllc.com

Kindness

Vol. 1

from the author

I am delighted that you have accepted the mission to be fruitful and multiply! Fruity Journals is a book series based on cultivating the fruit of God's Spirit in your life. In this journal, I share God inspired wisdom and life experiences that have pushed me closer to Him.

Fruity Journals will help the garden of your heart to flourish with peace, joy, kindness, gentleness, patience, faithfulness, self control, love and goodness. And God's word tells us that out of the abundance of the heart, the mouth speaks. You will witness God's fruit develop in your character, mind, and heart as this book takes you into the caverns of your life and offers you practical prompts for digging and soul searching.

This journal is for women just like you. Women who want to take their relationship deeper with God. Sometimes you have to go down before you can go up! Everyone likes to look at a pretty garden, but the truth is, it is messy. It is a process and every stage is not cute, but the results of health and beauty are to be treasured.

Sometimes, our gardens are nurtured by storms. The next time you go through one of life's storms, you can have the supernatural peace that keeps your mind and heart at ease. This journal series offers you daily tools to brighten your inner light and color your life with the vibrancy of God's goodness.

Okay, that is enough from me. This is the start of your spiritual self care journey.

AMBER JOY THAXTON, LPC

⁹Let love be without deceit. Be haters of what is evil; keep your minds fixed on what is good. ¹⁰Be **kind** to one another with a brother's love, putting others before yourselves in honour; ¹¹Be not slow in your work, but be quick in spirit, as the Lord's servants;

Romans 12:9-11 BBE

DAY 1

Kindness is often mistaken as a nice gesture.

Nice is likened to a behavior, whereas kindness is sourced from a genuine loving nature. We want our nature, our impulses, and instincts to be shaped and developed by the powerful abundance of God's love.

Kindness Prayer:

Lord, help us to examine the motives of our love.
Adapt our hearts and thoughts to what is right and pure.
We want the brotherly affection You had for Your disciples
that enabled You to see past their faults and see them as
worthy of respect, kindness, and relationship with You.
God, equip Your servants with a Christ-like attitude
and actions that follow.

"In an outburst of anger I hid My face from you for a moment, but with everlasting loving **kindness** I will have compassion on you," says the Lord your Redeemer.

Isaiah 54:8 NASB

DAY 2

God, You are truth, and You keep it real with me.
You deserve the same from me.

Forgive me for the times I have provoked Your anger through
moments of pride or disobedience. I acknowledge that I
fall short of perfection, and **it is Your everlasting love and
kindness that opens the door for forgiveness** and do-overs.

It is You and only You that can redeem me.

God thank you for your grace
and mercy. Thank you for loving
me despite of me. Teach me
to be more like you. To show
more compassion, more grace,
more love, more kindness.
cover my family,
protect my peace,
draw me nearer,
     Amen,
          Torie♡

it is Your
~~everlasting~~
~~love~~ and
kindness
that opens
the door for
forgiveness

³¹Let all bitterness and wrath and anger and clamor and slander be put away from you, along with all malice. ³²Be **kind** to one another, tenderhearted, forgiving one another, as God in Christ forgave you.

Ephesians 4:31–32 ESV

³¹Let all bitterness and wrath and anger and clamor and slander be put away from you, along with all malice. ³²Be **kind** to one another, tenderhearted, forgiving one another, as God in Christ forgave you.

Ephesians 4:31–32 ESV

`/2/23`

S M T W ~~T~~ F S

it is Your

~~everlasting~~

~~love~~ and

kindness

that opens

the door for

forgiveness

³⁵But love your enemies, and do good, and lend, expecting nothing in return, and your reward will be great, and you will be sons of the Most High, for he is **kind** to the ungrateful and the evil. ³⁶Be merciful, even as your Father is merciful.

Luke 6:35-36 ESV

DAY 4

This passage is not some goodhearted act of kindness.
This is an act of God! Get in your mind a person that has harmed you.
(Now, this may take a minute if you have succeeded in being fully
present at this moment, but let's just go there for a minute).
Now this may be someone that has opposed you by slander or deed.
Whatever the case, try to focus your mind on them. Keep that person
in your mind as you imagine yourself offering them a smile and a
gesture of goodwill while they maintain their usual countenance.

Okay, what was that like?

If we are any kin, then this exercise was a failure. I gave a glance
and quickly opted out by turning away. But the Bible reminds me, "I can
do all things through Christ." So next time, we are going to practice
putting on the armor of God before we face this giant of a task.
As we stand in the dressing room of our faith, let's pick up and put on
each piece of armor necessary for obedience. First and foremost,
we put on the helmet of salvation so we can get our minds right.

Next, let's put on the breastplate of righteousness to protect our
tender hearts. Next, snap on that belt of truth that keeps us
centered in truth. As we move down, let's grab those
shoes of peace that God uses to lead us along still waters.

Grab that shield of faith that keeps back the lies of the enemy.
And last but not least, the sword of the Spirit that sets us apart from mediocrity
and spearheads our supernatural ability to look at and divide our enemy.
Leaving on one side the person and on the other side the deed that hurt us.

Because of God, we can hate the sin and love the sinner.
For we are all sinners saved by Grace.

But the fruit of the Spirit is love, joy, peace, patience, **kindness,** goodness, faithfulness, gentleness, self-control; against such things there is no law.

Psalm 28:7 NIV

DAY 5

Laws are codes of conduct that dictate behavior.

God sent Jesus so that we could be in a relationship with Him.
The beauty that is birthed from our relationship with
God are things that are out of this world, such as
love, joy, peace, patience, kindness, goodness,
faithfulness, gentleness, and self-control.
The world can't give it, and the world can't take it away.

The world does, however, get to benefit from the fruit that
comes from our lives because we said yes to Jesus.
Do not consider the evangelism of your lifestyle small.
Actions speak louder than words.

Which fruit comes easiest for you?
Which one would you like to see grow more this season?

⁴But God, being rich in mercy, because of the great love with which he loved us, ⁵even when we were dead in our trespasses, made us alive together with Christ—by grace you have been saved— ⁶and raised us up with him and seated us with him in the heavenly places in Christ Jesus, ⁷so that in the coming ages he might show the immeasurable riches of his grace in **kindness** toward us in Christ Jesus.

Ephesians 2:4-7 ESV

DAY 6

What a Cinderella story!
God is the best fit for us.

He has everything, He knows everything, and He has all the
power. He saw you before your glow up, and He did not
offer a donation or handout. **He offered us a life with Him.**
All so He could show off His boundless wealth of
generosity and love to you forever.

When you are aware of your shortcomings, believing that you
are deserving of this kind of love is tough to swallow.
But this is not about what you think or feel. This is about
accepting the truth. And God says you're worthy!

What do you say?

He offered us a life with him.

Whoever pursues righteousness and **kindness** will find life, righteousness, and honor.

Proverbs 21:21 NIV

DAY 7

Righteousness requires us to walk with God
and realize that we have to get recentered every day.

As you spend time with God on a daily basis, recenter
yourself in God by washing yourself with the word.
God says you're worthy. Next, clothe yourself with the
garment of praise as you offer worship to God.

Here, you will find true freedom.

[a]Love is patient and **kind;** love does not envy or boast; it is not arrogant [5]or rude. It does not insist on its own way; it is not irritable or resentful;[a] [6]it does not rejoice at wrongdoing, but rejoices with the truth. [7]Love bears all things, believes all things, hopes all things, endures all things.

1 Corinthians 13:4–7 ESV

DAY 8

Read the passage.

Take the word love and replace it with your name.

_____ is patient and kind;

_____ does not envy or boast;

_____ is not arrogant or rude.

_____ does not insist on its own way;

_____ is not irritable or resentful;

_____ does not rejoice at wrongdoing,

but rejoices with the truth.

_____ bears all things, believes all things,

hopes all things, endures all things.

Make this your confession today!

A man who is **kind** benefits himself, but a cruel man hurts himself.

Proverbs 11:17 ESV

DAY 9

A guilty conscience crowds the mind.

When we make choices that take others' into consideration,
we add to the peace and harmony in our own lives.

Take a moment to think about someone in your life and ask
yourself how you could show consideration for them today.

He has told you, O man, what is good; and what does the LORD require of you but to do justice, and to love **kindness,** and to walk humbly with your God?

Micah 6:8 ESV

DAY 10

Let's be grateful for the clarity God has given us.

He is upfront about what He wants for us.
No matter what it feels like, we can please God.
I know it can feel like no matter what you do,
it is not good enough for God.
But God is good enough by Himself.

He is simply directing us to take His hand,
to be fair in our dealings, and to revive our
hearts with compassion and generosity.

Good job, sis!

You have chosen
to water your seed!

Write down 3 areas where you are expecting a harvest.

_____

_____

_____

Thus says the LORD of hosts, Render true judgments, show **kindness** and mercy to one another, do not oppress the widow, the fatherless, the sojourner, or the poor, and let none of you devise evil against another in your heart.

Zechariah 7:9-10 ESV

DAY 11

This verse alone seems pretty easy to accept.
God instructs us to be kind to everyone.

Interestingly, this message comes from a Prophet to a
people who had cherry-picked how they would serve God.
They opted to fast from food rather than honor others.

Showing the love of Christ is easy when you are
looking in a mirror. It is when we turn toward
others that it can become challenging.

For whom do you need to partner
with God to show kindness?

²³Have nothing to do with foolish, ignorant controversies; you know that they breed quarrels. ²⁴And the Lord's servant must not be quarrelsome but **kind** to everyone, able to teach, patiently enduring evil, ²⁵correcting his opponents with gentleness. God may perhaps grant them repentance leading to a knowledge of the truth, ²⁶and they may come to their senses and escape from the snare of the devil after being captured by him to do his will.

2 Timothy 2:23-26 ESV

DAY  12

In a culture that has embraced pettiness, we have seen
the climate of drama and disrespect boomerang beyond
reality TV, past politics, and do a full sweep
through many of our churches.

No one is exempt from the desire to do what pleases their
flesh in a moment, even when it is at the cost of others.
God is not asking us to be passive and avoid conflict.
God is instructing us on how to avoid holding our own and
pick up the responsibility of upholding His character.

God has chosen to make His home in us.
He has given us instructions on teaching others with our
actions as we diffuse confrontation and demonstrate
kindness through gentleness and patience.

How can you use God's message today
in adjusting your approach to confrontation?

¹You, therefore, have no excuse, you who pass judgment on someone else, for at whatever point you judge another, you are condemning yourself, because you who pass judgment do the same things. ²Now we know that God's judgment against those who do such things is based on truth. ³So when you, a mere human being, pass judgment on them and yet do the same things, do you think you will escape God's judgment? ⁴Or do you show contempt for the riches of his kindness, forbearance and patience, not realizing that God's **kindness** is intended to lead you to repentance?

Romans 2:1-4 NIV

DAY 13

So, in other words, do not be a hypocrite.

It is human nature to see someone else's actions as worse than your own. For when we practice the same lude act, we have the backstory that helps to create a little understanding of the error. What the passage reminds us of in Romans is that God is the one who holds the ruler. Only He can provide us with any measure of judgment.

When we attempt to hold the measuring stick, we'll inevitably fumble the riches of God's kindness, grace, and patience which we desperately need in order to walk out a Godly life.

DATE: / / S M T W T F S

³For we ourselves were once foolish, disobedient, led astray, slaves to various passions and pleasures, passing our days in malice and envy, hated by others and hating one another. ⁴But when the goodness and loving **kindness** of God our Savior appeared, ⁵He saved us, not because of works done by us in righteousness, but according to His own mercy, by the washing of regeneration and renewal of the Holy Spirit.

Titus 3:3-5 ESV

DAY 14

Thank you, Lord, for entering my life and making it new.
It was trash without you!
That's my story in a nutshell. LOL.

Can you recall the moment that God came on the scene of
your life? The moment you experienced kindness instead of
wrath. What about one of the times He saved you instead of
kicking you while you were down?

No matter who you are or what you have done, God's
presence in your life has the ability to power wash away all
the guilt, shame, and pain you have ever experienced.

If you have never experienced this, now is the time!
Invite God in right now and be honest with
Him about your shortcomings.

With an open heart and outstretched arms, surrender to the
gentle shower of His mercy that will rejuvenate you today!

...but let him who boasts, boast of this, that he understands and knows Me, that I am the Lord who exercises **lovingkindness,** justice and righteousness on earth; for I delight in these things," declares the Lord.

Jeremiah 9:24 NIV

DAY 15

The only thing worth bragging about is the approval of our adoption into the family of God.

Take a few minutes to write a gratitude list of God's character that you have witnessed.

You have granted me life and **lovingkindness;** And Your care has preserved my spirit.

Job 10:12 ESV

DAY 16

The unconditional love and generosity of the Lord are granted.

Grants are different than loans in that they are gifts that are not expected to be returned. What God has granted us feels less supplemental and more vital than anything. God shows up in a way for us that no bank account or gift ever could.

Take a moment to think about a time God came through and granted you something you did not deserve.

Now, shake the urge to repay Him and take a moment to praise Him!

She opens her mouth with wisdom and the teachings of **kindness** are on her tongue.

Proverbs 31:26 NIV

DAY 17

How many times have you heard the phrase,
"If you don't have anything nice to say,
do not say anything at all."?

As a mother, I recognize that some
lessons are better taught at the level of the recipient.
Now that I am teaching my little ones how to
communicate more efficiently, I am careful to make
sure my words build up my children and those around me.

Someone once told me people do not always remember what
you said, but they will remember how you made them feel.
I know that God has made me feel secure and cared for.
Maybe you don't remember what last week's sermon was
about, but can you recall how you felt as the
Minister taught about the Lord?

Describe the impression you want to leave with others today?

He is a tower of salvation and great deliverance to His king, And shows **lovingkindness** to His anointed, To David and his offspring forever.

2 Samuel 22:51 AMP

DAY 18

In times of shame and guilt, a place to go and be restored is the only atmosphere we can allow ourselves to be seen fully.

When we enter the tower of deliverance, imagine God is waiting with anticipation with open arms in the foyer. Strip down, get out of those dirty secrets, and peel off the mask of fear. You are safe with Him.

Better is one day in His house than a thousand elsewhere.

Wherever you imagine 'elsewhere' being better (status, income bracket, marriage, the past), just know that no place compares to where you stand with God!

Better is one
day in His
house than
a thousand
elsewhere.

the LORD was with him; he showed him **kindness** and granted him favor in the eyes of the prison warden.

Genesis 39:21 NIV

DAY 19

Joseph, who came from an elevated position,
found himself in the cross hairs of the prison warden.

He was probably a little, no, a lot, outside his comfort zone.
God wants us to know that whatever situation we find
ourselves in, we are never too far from the reach of
His favor or the comfort of His presence.

Dismiss the lies, shame and whispers from the shadows
and trust and believe that God sees you and nothing
can keep you from His kind love and favor.

"The LORD bless him!" Naomi said to her daughter-in-law. "He has not stopped showing his **kindness** to the living and the dead." She added, "That man is our close relative; he is one of our guardian-redeemers."

Ruth 2:20 NIV

DAY 20

A woman who has outlived her spouse and children knows
pain that the Grand Canyon lacks the capacity to withstand.

Like a rock shifted in the caverns, acts of kindness
go undetected in the abyss of our deepest pain.
Accepting kindness when we are hurting deeply is not easy.
But God does not desire for us to hurt alone. If you find
yourself in a season of grief, take all the time you need,
because life will never be as you have known it.

Remember that taking time for yourself is different from
isolation. The difference can be recognized as a trait.
Time to oneself is characterized by connection with oneself.
Isolation intends to disconnect you completely.
This means disconnection from others, and from
your own thoughts and emotions.

In times of pain, do you find yourself running from others
or gravitating toward those who can support you?

Real

change

starts...

...beneath

the

surface.

16that He would grant you, according to the riches of His glory, to be strengthened with power through His Spirit in the inner [a]self, 17so that Christ may dwell in your hearts through faith; and that you, being rooted and grounded in love, 18may be able to comprehend with all the [b]saints what is the width and length and height and depth, 19and to know the love of Christ which surpasses knowledge, that you may be filled to all the fullness of God.

Ephesians 3:16-19 NASB

DAY 21

Have you ever felt the wear and tear on your mind from
staying up late running through the "what if" scenarios?
Or the depletion of hope after a rejection like
a breakup or a career detour?

There are times when you will feel worn down by life, and
there is no beverage or amount of money that can restore your
joy like Jesus. God's care can't fit in a package.

The book of Ephesians describes it best as it excuses the
possibility of reducing God's love down to anything we
have a scale for. The care God provides is supernatural.
It has the power to bring the dead back to life.

Wither no longer!
Speak life over your mind, body, and spirit today.
Declare that your life is restored, hope is replenished,
and your needs are met by God.

When our ancestors were in Egypt, they gave no thought to your miracles; they did not remember your many **kindnesses,** and they rebelled by the sea, the Red Sea.

Psalms 106:7 NIV

DAY 22

There are some things you just have to see to believe it.

And there are plenty of times God has displayed His power through taking actions in our lives. The key to a secure walk with God, whom you may not see with your eyes, is to remember in your mind how He has revealed Himself time and time again.

Take a moment to write about a time that…
• A need got provided.
• Someone offered you something you did not deserve.
• You felt God's supernatural presence.
• Peace entered your heart when the circumstances had not quite changed.

8 [a]To sum up, all of you be harmonious, sympathetic, [b] loving, compassionate, and humble; 9 not returning evil for evil or insult for insult, but giving a blessing instead; for you were called for the very purpose that you would inherit a blessing.

10 For, "The one who desires life, to love and see good days, Must keep his tongue from evil and his lips from speaking deceit.

11 He must turn away from evil and do good; He must seek peace and pursue it.

12 For the eyes of the Lord are toward the righteous, and His ears attend to their prayer, But the face of the Lord is against evildoers."

1 Peter 3:8-12 NASB

DAY 23

Payback should be nothing less than a blessing!

1 Peter 3:8-12 defines kindness in such raw detail that no matter who reads it, there is something to strive toward. Peter lays out the blueprint of what a godly approach to kindness looks like.

What parts in this passage do you need the help of God to perform?

DATE: / /   S   M   T   W   T   F   S

Your **kindness** will reward you, but your cruelty will destroy you.

Proverbs 11:17 NLT

DAY 24

Read this passage carefully.

Notice how both cruelty and kindness are ours.
You are capable of both.
It's your job to get them both out of you.

Which one will you dispose of?
Which one will you offer?

S   M   T   W   T   F   S

But love your enemies, do good to them, and lend to them without expecting to get anything back. Then your reward will be great, and you will be children of the Most High, because he is **kind** to the ungrateful and wicked.

Luke 6:35 NIV

DAY  25

The more I walk with Christ, the more I realize
that I need Him EVERY step of the way.

Now is a good time to search your heart and surrender to
God any thoughts, agenda, or motives that do not align
with this passage from Luke. It's easy to be kind to those
who will smile back at you and agree with your politics.
The world does that. God is asking us to be over
the top with our love and generosity.

To be honest with you, my love falls short the
majority of the time. True love is to love others with
the love provided from the Savior. This type of love has no
take backs, no interest accrued, and no qualifications.

Love like Christ.

Love like
Christ.

¹³Let us behave properly as in the day, not in carousing and drunkenness, not in sexual promiscuity and sensuality, not in strife and jealousy. ¹⁴But put on the Lord Jesus Christ, and make no provision for the flesh in regard to its lusts.

Romans 13:13-14 NASB

DAY 26

Prayer:

Dear Lord, I come before You today and honor You.
You are all things beautiful, and You are worthy of all praise.
My desire is to obey You and make You proud.

There are some things You ask of me that seem impossible.
Blessing someone who has hurt, betrayed, slandered
my name, or rejected me can feel like a big ask.

Being empathetic, compassionate, and living in harmony
sounds easy when I feel like it. But Lord, I know I can do all
things through Your son, who has empowered me with His
strength. I leave my righteous anger with You. And I will bow
my head and open my hands for You to work through me.

The islanders showed us unusual **kindness.** They built a fire and welcomed us all because it was raining and cold.

Acts 28:2 NIV

DAY 27

Come to think of it, true kindness is unusual.

It is taking a step away from your important agenda
and moving in the direction of someone else's interest.
It is the act of being aware of others and paying
attention to the needs of those around you.

Be unusual today.
Differentiate yourself from the world
around you by reaching out to others!

Be unusual today.

Gracious words are a honeycomb, sweet to the soul and healing to the bones.

Proverbs 16:24 NIV

DAY 28

We live in a world with information overload.

Knowing when to add to the conversation is wisdom.
May self-control, patience, and peace be your guide.

At the opportune time, I pray others
experience you as a fresh spring of kindness.

Therefore, as God's chosen people, holy and dearly loved, clothe yourselves with compassion, **kindness,** humility, gentleness and patience.

Colossians 3:12 NIV

DAY 29

It's fascinating the words used to reflect God's
restorative power. He does not seek to destroy us.

He sees us as His masterpiece that just needs some dusting
off. God doesn't make junk. You cannot be replaced.

Whether you have a closet full of skeletons or you
are someone who has not lived a lot of life yet,
you are in desperate need of a power wash.

This world is full of the smog of idolatry, the pollution of
hate, and the litter of the enemies' lies that get into all our
heads from time to time. But thank God for His kindness and
love that saves us through the supernatural cleaning power
that restores us to original preciousness. Receive it today.

Recite it with me.
I am precious.

Whoever is **kind** to the poor lends to the Lord, and he will reward them for what they have done.

Proverbs 19:17 NIV

DAY 30

Kindness comes in all forms, shapes, and sizes.

Take a moment to think about how you can
give generously to those around you?
(Donations, volunteer, give, share, encourage).

You are blessed to be a blessing.

Trust that God will continue to supply
all of your needs according to His wealth.

You are
~~blessed~~ to
be a blessing.

My heart is good soil.

Each day with the
help of the Holy Spirit,
I survey my heart.

I believe when I confess
my sins, I am forgiven.

I believe when I cast
my cares, I am free.

Day after day, God
replenishes me from
His well of living water.

And as a result, my
life is blossoming
with Godly fruit.

Amen.

CPSIA information can be obtained
at www.ICGtesting.com
Printed in the USA
JSHW070903180123
36364JS00001B/1